EVERYDAY EXPERIENCES TO IMPROVE YOUR WORK AND LIFE

REFLECTION STRATEGIES FROM A MOTIVATIONAL LEADER

Author: Dr. Gary Damon, Jr.
Foreword: Mr. DeShawn A. King, M.A.

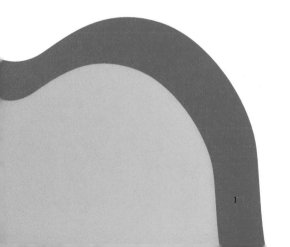

Manufactured in the United States of America

Cataloging-in-Publication data for this book is available from the Library of Congress

ISBN-13: 978-1-7352637-2-4

FIRST EDITION –

Illustrations: Courtney Monday

Editing: WesCourt Advisors

USA $ 15.99

ACKNOWLEDGEMENT

Thank you to the following people that helped me throughout this journey.

Publisher: Johnson Tribe Publishing House, LLC (JTP)
Illustrator: Courtney Monday
Company: Pressure Point Consulting, LLC

DEDICATION

This book is dedicated to the millions of people working to balance work and life. You are the real MVPs!

FOREWORD

Walking with the right people adds electricity and energy to conversations. I walked many domestic and international roads with Dr. Damon. Everyday experiences were discovered during one of these walks that eventually moved Gary to write this book. In this book, you will learn how an experience removes you from your current situation and encourages you to establish creative outcomes. Always know there are no limits to thinking.

Very proud of you, Gary!

DeShawn A. King, M.A.

INTRODUCTION

Life has ebbs and flows that require us to take pause, gather our thoughts, and make decisions to get us back to where we need to be. We experience so much in one day that we forget to think about anything else aside from stressors, barriers, and what we must do next. Slowing down is not in the foreseeable future; therefore, everyday experiences are helpful to adjust thinking, manage behaviors, and produce positive outcomes.

Similar to our family life, our work life has some of the same features shared above, would you agree? The workplace causes us to take pause, recalibrate, adjust accordingly, make the most appropriate decision and move on. Has this ever happened to you at work? Think about the mundane things in our essential duties we often overlook, yet we do each day, i.e. checking our emails, sharing a story with a colleague, or walking down the hallway from your office to the bathroom and back. Maybe, some of these routine experiences are just what you may need to keep you going and allow you to, maybe, pivot from the broken relationship or shattered friendship that left you scarred with a void.

Believe it or not, ordinary, routine, typical and commonplace experiences have helped me become better at decision making, collaborating with colleagues, leading teams of people, and most importantly, balancing my work and my life. There was a moment in time where I was losing focus, so one day I came to realize that the very things I experience everyday helped me look at my role differently. When I finally listened for intent with purpose, I began to learn there are many everyday experiences that have shaped my perspective: experiences like brushing my teeth, walking up the stairs, washing the dishes, and so on.

Workplace challenges, difficult decisions, and juggling the daily grind is tough and sometimes hard to handle. This book will give you an edge in how best to balance and manage your personal and professional lives.

Just like life, the following summaries are not written in any particular order, rather, they are categorized and can be read any day, anyway, and applied any time. Choose any summary, read and apply it and let me know what you think. If you can't use it, share it with a family member, friend, or colleague, or someone close to you.

INSTRUCTIONS WITH INTENTION

I recall my former pastor sharing with me "change only happens when you happen to change." The many lessons I gleaned from this eight-word statement have helped me withstand some of the many challenges at home and in the workplace. For instance, as an up-and-coming leader, I always felt that dictating my directions would get the desired results. Oh, how I learned rather quickly that was not the case! After several failed attempts of leading with an iron fist, I had to change my behavior toward a more inclusive and integrated approach. With time, I began leading teams toward high performance, increasing morale, and surpassing goals.

Over the next several pages you will take a journey with me and gain deeper insights, consider outside-the-box perspectives, and mature into new approaches that will allow you to manage and handle your work differently. The summaries in Everyday Experiences are meant to help you embrace the moment you are in, find words to summarize how you feel, and offer questions for you to answer.

These questions are specific for each experience and are expected to be answered with open integrity. There will be moments where you are encouraged to illustrate how you feel. You do not have to be the best artist, yet, give it the good old college try.

On the contrary, there are some experiences that may have a scenario to encourage you to examine how it is relevant and real in your current workplace. As you know, the workplace is a very tricky place to be in without being properly equipped with tools and strategies to help you and everyone around you to win!

When I started writing about things I was uncomfortable sharing aloud, I better understood that was the area that I needed to change! Over time I learned that establishing my voice, growing my intuition, and drowning out the noise were the very things I needed to deploy to be an effective leader. I want you to consider and put into action these three takeaways and the many experiences you will read.

TABLE OF CONTENTS

RANDALL'S MODEL

I remember the episode on *This Is Us* where Randall and some of his political peers were playing golf and he played poorly. At the end of the scene Randall returned to the golf course and played much better. He did not show his strength until he learned the agenda of others and which skills he would need in order to succeed. Similar to Randall's response in the scene ought to be deployed by us at some of our toughest moments to make decisions at work and home.

At work, we encounter diverse people with different motives and end goals. As such, we must always remain vigilant and keep a close eye to determine their motives. There are several ways people may approach you daily, i.e. collaborating on a winning proposal, changing careers, compromising your integrity, and so on.

From experience, the following tactics may be useful for you in order to make the best decision to either remain with them or find the right off ramp to move out and move on! Consider the following:

- be inquisitive (ask open-ended questions to gain their in sight)
- stay engaged (smile through the conversation, repeat back any pertinent information)
- and, never show your cards until you have the end results (keep your information tight until you are ready to share!)

If you employ the above techniques in your daily interactions, you will have everything required to make your next best move with healthy and more informed decisions. Always remain active and know you got this.

1. Where have you seen this in your workplace?

2. What steps will you take to make a better decision next time?

3. What could have been avoided? Talked out?

WAYNES OF THE WORLD

Being taken advantage of is never easy to see, but it is always hard to understand. Have you ever worked hard on a project with co-workers, classmates or others and in the end they take full credit? Or have you spent a great deal of time developing a winning proposal to share with your boss, but you wanted to discuss it with your colleague first? Waynes of the world are the people that will take all of the credit and leave no room for you to shine. At first, Waynes of the world will seem friendly, professional, and concerned about you, yet they will use you for their gain. To avoid being a victim of the Waynes of the world, create boundaries and work to stay ahead of them. When you create boundaries, you are allowing yourself the space to consider which angle your colleague or peer is coming from, in turn, will help you stay ahead of them. In one of my first teaching jobs I learned that a lesson plan idea I shared with a former colleague was later used during his mid-year observation. As you may imagine, I was upset and considered it a lesson learned. Unfortunately, I did not learn that lesson until years later. Being the victim to the Waynes of the world will continue to happen until you decide to create boundaries and find workarounds that will help you stay ahead of them.

1. Can you identify specifically how you fell victim to the Waynes of the world? What was the specific situation? How did you manage and overcome this experience? In what professional setting did you experience this type of behavior?

2. How often do you find yourself in a Wayne's world? How do you make a graceful exit?

3. When this behavior happens again, what will you do differently to avoid being victimized?

LAZY INCOMPETENCE

You work with people who will do as little as possible but have so much to say about everything. These are the same people that will speak up to help solve complex problems and will not willingly volunteer to stay late to finish a work project. These are the same people that will work to spend more time telling you what to do and what is required to change processes and behaviors, rather than working together toward desired results and noticeable solutions. They are lazy on purpose and incompetent by accident.

As you consider the moments where you have identified in yourself and maybe others wherein Lazy Incompetence played out, be sure to understand some leading behaviors by considering the following definitions:

1. Lazy- not willing to put much effort or energy into an activity or task
2. Incompetence- not showing or demonstrating the required skills to be successful at a job or in their profession

Scenario

Marty is the co-worker with more than ten years with the organization and less than four in your department. He believes his years of experience affords him the opportunity to manage people and projects and less time actually doing things. Marty is always your supervisor's go-to person on projects; therefore, he believes he is the supervisor. Unfortunately, Marty spends more time telling you and everyone around you what to do. Marty overheard your supervisor advising next steps to your report that is due by close of business. Instead of Marty focusing on his own report, he decides to spend additional time repeating (in different words) what was just shared with you. Lazy incompetence is at play when less energy is present for Marty to self-reflect and work on his own report, however, he decides to focus on you and your work.

Takeaways

After reading this everyday experience and the scenario, what are some key takeaways? From experience, 1.) Not everyone that speaks makes sense, 2.) Regardless of what you do, people will be themselves, therefore, be the best version of you! 3.) When you try and it did not work, try again!

SHOW YOUR TEETH

When you have nothing else to give and you are expected to challenge the normal everyday nuisances of work, be sure people understand this behavior. There are people who think they have the power to control you. If you give them that power, they will control you. There will come a time where you must show your teeth. For instance, you are in the minority of a decision and you have evidence to back up your claims, you show your teeth and stick to your decision. I recall the hiring team and I were torn between two really good candidates: one had more years of experience and less education, while the other had more education and less years of experience. I suggested we hire the individual with less experience so we may train and teach him the proper skills on the job. Being the manager had its perks that day and we hired him and he turned out to be a quality staff and was later promoted to supervisor.

By showing your teeth, you are demonstrating to others a piece of you and that you can take just as much as they can give. When you have to show your teeth to get what you are destined for helps you make more enhanced and experienced decisions. When you show your teeth, you are giving people one perspective with a realistic approach. Too often people believe their decision is the right decision until you paint a picture that is compelling and makes sense.

I remember my grandmother always shared 'proof is in the pudding;' in this case it is in your teeth!

Confession 1

I was in the minority when it came to terminating an employee. Based on my experience with the individual, their work productivity, and lackluster approach was hindering the performance of the department. My supervisor felt that I did not have enough documentation to support my claim; therefore, my lack of information hindered my ability to terminate the employee. In this instance, I showed my teeth and failed. Fast forward to today, not only am I taking better notes, I have a different approach in handling delicate situations such as this and that is providing professional coaching, matching the employee up with a mentor, and giving them time to grow into their position.

1. After reading my confession, has something similar happened to you? If so, share a specific example.

2. Does 'stop, look, and take action' help or hinder you when you attempt to show your teeth?

3. After reading the example in the experience above, how would you respond to these questions?
Demonstrating diligence is developed over time, based on this experience, where have you matured? Need to mature?

Now that you read through 'Show your Teeth' and answered the thought-provoking questions, I would like to share a second confession that helped me grow and mature with a different experience.

Confession 2

A former colleague was convinced that her methodology for sharing recruitment data per zip code by client intake forms only was the right process; however, it became clear we were not collecting applications at enrollment which reduced our funding by 10% after one quarter with a social learning grant. Instead of going with her process in Quarter Two, I decided to show my teeth and challenge her and later learned this new process was the easiest, so much so, it became the new process department-wide. This version of showing my teeth helped me gain the confidence at work and find my voice in tough moments.

Similarly, the next everyday experience helped give me the voice to speak up and allowed me space to grow in showing my teeth. A stair landing is a place where you dwell and decide between going up or coming down, regardless of the direction you will get to the right place.

STAIR LANDING

To take your best shot, big risk, or leap into your scariest decision to date, be sure you spend time at your stair landing. The stair landing affords you the opportunity to toss around intuitive ideas and consider different viewpoints necessary to help make informed and healthy decisions around complex problems. Since it is situated between levels, it helps you gain traction and breath before moving forward. This concept helps you deeply engage with your inner voice and allows you to understand what lies ahead. At the stair landing you are free from momentary distractions and you are less likely to be interrupted by outside noise. The next time you take the stairs, recognize the great benefits the landing affords you as you move toward the right answer to your best shot, big risk, or scariest decision.

Scenario

You were offered a job in a different state. Your supervisor offered you a lateral promotion within the company, but in a different department. An opportunity with a competing agency presented itself, however, it was less pay and fewer hours, but provided more professional exposure. When scenarios like this happen but you are scared to take the leap and dive right into the situation; what do you do next? Should you consider this promotion? Stay with the same company? Decide whether to share your vulnerable thoughts with your boss about the budget? No worries, the stair landing is the right experience to help you gather your thoughts!

Confession 1

Prior to my stair landing experience, I considered general details about my performance and accomplishments, but after my stair landing experience, I constructed an outline of achievements and targets of impact to demonstrate why I deserved a promotion. I was less nervous bringing this to my supervisor's attention because my time on the stair landing allowed me to process my thoughts, determine my motives, and conceptualize my plan. This approach allowed me to understand and appreciate pausing in the stairwell for I had time to plan my proposal and reflect on my reward.

Below is an example of the outline of achievements and targets of impact.

TARGETS OF IMPACT AND AREAS OF ACHIEVEMENT

MONTH 1	• Improved team communication by sharing weekly emails of highlights, staff success stories, and performance losses/gains • Spent time surveying each staff one by one to determine individual and team strengths • Re-established weekly staff huddles and incorporated a team activity

MONTH 3	• Increased team morale and office culture • Spent time surveying stakeholders and community members to determine needs and wants • Rebranded the team's vision and goals
MONTH 6	• Researched and explored grant opportunities to increase service delivery • Updated the team's performance metrics to align with promising growth opportunities • Increased the team by hiring three new staff that will balance the workload
ONE YEAR	• Increased the department's total operating budget from $375,000 to $598,000 in one year. • Intentionally promoted one staff to shift leader • Team morale and office culture remains high

Activity

Can you think of a workplace situation that requires you to spend time on your stair landing at home? If so, muster up two or three responses to that situation, take your best one and share it with your boss. With this workplace situation draw two sets of stairs going up and going down. Between each stair you will have a landing. In the landing space come up with two or three SMART (Specific, Meaningful, Attainable, Realistic, and Time-sensitive) goals. Your smart goals should capture short- and long-term objectives you wish to see come to fruition in your current role. Hang this some place you will see it often.

Below you will find an example of how I captured short-term and long term goals that I hoped for in one of my previous team's I managed.

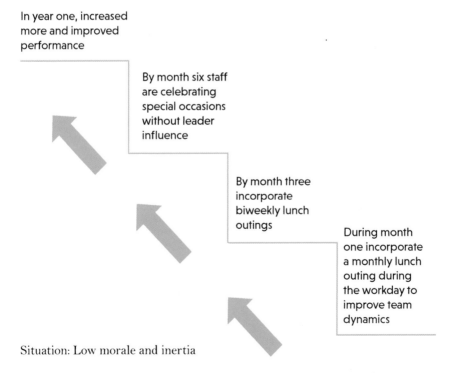

In year one, increased more and improved performance

By month six staff are celebrating special occasions without leader influence

By month three incorporate biweekly lunch outings

During month one incorporate a monthly lunch outing during the workday to improve team dynamics

Situation: Low morale and inertia

CLOSET CHAT WITH THE DOOR CLOSED

While stair landings provide an open opportunity to process thoughts and share with others, on the contrary, a closet chat with the door closed allows you to hunker down and spend much needed individual quality time to regain control. Closets are a closed, confined space where you are searching for something to wear, organizing supplies, or storing items. This is generally the place where it is okay to speak to yourself and gather thoughts about particular subjects or dicey situations at hand. Closets hold items we desire to store for later use, just like our thoughts. The closet is a short experience where you regain a lot of insight and intuition to help you along the way. Subsequently, the stair landing helps you grow outwardly while your moments with the closet chat with the door closed offers you time to process, proceed, and pave the way.

Scenario

You are preparing annual performance appraisals for each staff on your team. The next section, time and attendance stirs up agitated emotions for you slacked off considerably on this policy with five top performing staff. Because of this you are now stuck how to handle this situation. You recall several months ago your supervisor made you aware she noticed your inconsistencies, but, you never made any noteworthy changes about it. You are now torn in a few places. What are your next steps? How will you manage this situation? The closet chat with the door closed is a great way to help you to consider alternative options with possible solutions. Finally, the lesson learned in this experience is for us to understand that broken expectations breed natural consequences.

1. Where do you go for sound, healthy advice? Explain where it helped you and how it helped you.

2. Over the next two days, share your best closet decision-making experience with someone and ask what they would have done differently, if anything.

3. What strategies will you use to handle your next closet chat?

PRESSURE IS A PRIVILEGE

Pressure comes in all shapes and sizes; therefore, we cannot handle it the same every time. You may be an entry-level staff trying to arrive on time to work after taking three buses and walking a quarter of a mile, barely stepping your feet on the company's front doors just to hear once more "you are late!" This overwhelming, stressful feeling happens to just about everyone in the workforce, past and present. You may demonstrate you are okay, deep down you are upset and ready to quit and give up!

Maybe, you are the emerging leader who struggles with attention to detail. Your overall performance in program development, operations, people-centered approaches, and strong positive leadership qualities are exceptional, however, your attention to detail still is underwhelming.

Next time you encounter situations similar to the illustrations above, remember you are built for this kind of pressure. Oh, when you are making strides to move past these pressures, life or circumstances will get much tougher before you may share your testimony. Just know that pressure really is a privilege.

Scenario

Your department is faced with eliminating six of thirteen positions because of the 13% reduction in your overall operating budget. Just like me, you believe every position is vital and plays a key role in the success of the team. Your supervisor disagrees and tasked you with coming up with a new staffing structure. You are also asked to lead the discussion with your team once your plan is finalized. This pressure is real and often felt when you are at your most successful place.

Confession

During one of my first workplace crises as a supervisor, I failed miserably in managing the crisis and the steps that followed. It was tough to lead a team, manage performance, submit reports, adhere to policies and procedures, coach and discipline staff for poor performance and at times unruly decorum, attend meetings, all while trying to remain level-headed. Over time, I learned the skills and competencies required to lead and manage teams toward teamwork, performance, and mentorship. Transferable skills and activities like those above helped me prioritize problems that would always lead me to manage people first, then the problem, and end up with the most suitable plan toward the desired outcomes. Later, everyday experiences like this helped me establish several useful best practices that taught me to lead with a strength-based, transformational way.

> • Pressure is present all the time. Might I suggest you spend five minutes and meditate with the lights dimmed, eyes closed, and distractions on mute. Once your time is up, share how those five minutes made you feel.

THROWING A CHAIR
(FIGURATIVELY THINKING OR SPEAKING)

In a rage, people will say something they will regret and do something they will later have to pay the price. The act of chair-throwing gives you the ability to take all of your present energy and throw it as hard and as possible. Why? It provides us with the satisfaction that all of the stress went with the chair.

When you throw a chair, it gives you the flexibility to be free from all distractions. Your mind is more focused on the shattering noise and many broken pieces of glass you have to clean once you regain control. Chair-throwing is much like problem-solving; you are throwing out multiple options until you have the most suitable outcome. Your current issues are solvable, but you are unclear about fixing them. Chair throwing produces positive results because you are breaking the silence and upsetting the status quo. Never allow the chair you sit in today be the very crutch to keep you sitting there tomorrow. Chair throwing, every time, will upset the atmosphere and keep things interesting. This experience reminded me of an instance when a former direct report grieved a longtime vacation policy. During his one-on-one with me, he provided facts that demonstrated how he earned more time than he could take given the team's size. I took his concerns to our Human Resources team. Because he voiced his concerns the organization updated the policy and added two part-time roles to allow staff the opportunity to exercise their right to time off.

The shattering noise that I heard from my employee prompted me to share this concern with Human Resources. If I did not understand his passion during our encounter, I would have dismissed his concern or placed it on the back burner. Experiences like this helped shape and prepared me for future chair-throwing situations.

Scenario

You work for a mission-driven, performance-based non-profit that thrives off the customer's experience. You are required to survey each customer with the same three or four questions. The customers are growing weary of answering the same question week after week. You heard their noise and decided to change up some of the questions without going through the approval process. The customers are more excited and eager to respond to your questions, so much so, the results have enhanced your front office operations.

1. When was the last time you threw a chair? How did it make you feel? Are there any more chairs to throw before moving on to your next challenge?

2. What "chair" have you thrown or do you need to throw today? This week? This year?

3. How does chair throwing refresh your thinking?

HALLWAY WHISPERS

In those moments when you want to give in and give up you hear those small whispers in the hallway. The intended purpose of whispers is to stop you in your tracks to give you the guidance and foresight that you need. The hallway is the pass-through to your next goal, objective, and step. The whisper comes from the still small voice that captures your attention to help you not give up or grow weary. Always remember there is an entry and exit to hallways, even if you must go back the way you came. Because of my stair landing experience, I can appreciate hallway whispers to help make decisions. The stair landing gives me tangible actions, while the hallway whispers provide me the internal perseverance that leads toward the next decision.

Confession

After spending more than two years in a high profile, stressful, and complex role, I decided to take a break from senior leadership and focus on finishing my doctoral degree. After spending time in the hallway and listening to the whispers, my next decision was clear. I literally received my whisper in the hallway five years ago while working my part-time job. While walking down the hallway, I overheard Leo, one of the students, express to his parents how he wished there were more Mr. Gary's in China teaching students English. In that moment, a whisper entered into my head, "relocate to China, focus on saving money, finishing your doctoral degree, and travel the world." At that moment, I started to research and explore this outlandish idea that later became one of the best decisions I made in life.

1. Regardless of the hallway, what is something you are being led to? What is stopping you?

2. Challenge: Help someone that is at their professional or personal hallway and give them positive, hopeful whispers to get them toward an exit or entry. You may be thinking, "How do I know someone is even in the hallway?" That's a good question. The signs are not always apparent; however, your gut instinct will give you clues that will lead you toward asking the right questions and giving them the right whispers to make their decision. In no way are you expected to change their mind, however, you are giving them tips to lead them toward the decision just like Leo in my confession.

WALKING WITH THE
TRUTH IN YOUR POCKET

When you are armed with the facts and know what is right there is no need to be afraid of retaliation or rejection. The truth matters and is given to the right people in due time. You do what is right even when no one is looking and are prepared to fight for it in the end. The truth in your pocket will keep you from making dirty decisions with people that are a walking lie. Sometimes this truth is standing up for what you believe in. It can be speaking up on behalf of others. It could be sharing what is important for the team when no one else will be the voice of reason. Next time you are approached with telling the truth, be sure you do! Be right and be responsible.

Scenario

Robin expressed to her colleague that his poor attention to detail affects her ability to finish the grant writing process on most, if not all projects. The colleague responded back with harsh words; however, Robin supported her claim by sharing several instances where his poor attention to detail caused her to spend an average of additional 45 minutes fixing the errors.

1. Does the truth hurt? How?

2. What was that hard truth someone shared with you and how did you use it to help you? Or did it hinder you? Share why or why not.

WALKING THE DOG
WITHOUT A LEASH

Dogs rely on their owner to care for and protect them, especially when their owner walks them without a leash. As the nurturing owner, we must look down the street, on our sides, and behind us to keep us away from the potential threat of harm and danger. As the dog's owner and best friend, our perspective and matter of control make a difference. In theory, we are their voice and at times matter of reason. Because dog owners are given the awesome task and privilege in nurturing them, continue to walk your dog without a leash. Just be sure to stand clear of anticipated disruptions and distractions.

This experience of walking the dog without a leash helped me understand how transformational leadership works. It also gave me the confidence to know I led teams the best way I knew how until I matured into knowing better. For this reason, my definition of transformational leadership is different than most; I care for, nurture, grow, and understand staff needs before making a hasty and unnecessary decision.

With my years of non-traditional experience leading teams, I learned that transformational leadership is when the leader identifies a needed change, creates a vision through execution, remains inspirational and motivational during tough times, and understand that strengths and weaknesses are part of the transformative journey. For these reasons, leaders must train themselves to lead with care and manage teams of people with trust. Like this experience, a dog trusts that you will not walk them into harm's way; instead, you will prepare them for what lies ahead. As leaders, with or without a title, we are expected to lead people with integrity, character, and ensure we remain inclusive to our decisions, so our tomorrows are better!

Confessions

I enjoy and appreciate the autonomy to birth, create, share, and influence programs and projects from infancy to full execution and follow-up. Some annoyances that often pop-up and throw me off guard are the ones that I should have known. Over time, I learned that my best projects and initiatives were those I had complete autonomy over and the opportunity to lead teams toward high performance, increased morale, and continued and renewed buy-in of the mission and vision of the organization.

I recall the moment I was encouraged to find grant money to support the organization's targeted population; at-risk, vulnerable, justice-involved men and women. May I add some of the most dedicated, willing to learn and train people that I worked within the last decade.

Over the next month, I found a local foundation interested in supporting our mission to help increase awareness and capacity of teamwork, decision-making, essential job skills, and the importance of being open and honest helped us win this two-year grant.

Because of the dedicated service, my team offered daily, the human-centered approach of understanding the importance of premium customer service, to the mission-driven thinking allowed our team to meet and exceed our performance goals. .

HEAD-ON COLLISIONS

Driving on country backroads is quite scary. Most times they are two lane highways situated between tree lines, scattered houses, with little to no light in dark times. Your bright lights complemented with high beams are most helpful in the darkest parts at night. Night vision is that extra precision to look beyond the trees, cars in the distance, deer and other animals. In the workplace, you must always be prepared for whatever driving conditions you may encounter. Depending on your workplace, your driving conditions vary. They may range from a bad boss, lack of training, not enough time to complete projects, to a disgruntled customer. To know you are driving well and not concerned with head-on collisions, be sure to use your precise night vision with the help of high beams to keep you focused, fixed on your destination, and free from unnecessary distractions that may cause damage.

Furthermore, your night vision at work allows you the ability to visualize and understand different perspectives before making the final decision. Your night vision is most seen and often observed when you are in crisis mode leading to your greatest breakthrough. Just like collisions in your car, we are met with collisions in the workplace. I remember the time my peer and I did not see eye-to-eye on how to handle staff performance. I thought it was most feasible to place an employee on an action plan with

SMART goals for 60-days, while my peer wished to suspend the employee for one week without pay and allow them to return to work with an action plan with no follow-up.

As you can imagine, we collided in our approaches and unfortunately we never resolved the issue. We decided to share our approaches with our supervisor and he used parts of each approach by suspending the staff member for three days without pay and placed him on a 30-day action plan with two follow-up items. The good thing from that situation was the opportunity to share this everyday experience with you. I can imagine that you have a similar situation in your workplace or even your personal life.

Rest assured, we have all been in this place and, unfortunately, it will happen again. For the ideal way to manage head-on collisions at work, you may want to:

- · Identify the problem
- Establish solutions
- Speak it out
- Tweak where appropriate
- Implement

1. **How did you handle your most recent head-on collision?**

2. What would you do differently the next time?

3. If the five steps above do not work for you, what will? Write it out, try it with a few friends, and then maybe at work.

MOMENTS OF REST

Did you know resting is a core part of a balanced life? When we allow our body to recover from a tough loss, a terribly bad work day, or in between meetings, you are giving yourself time to replenish energy and recover from the situation. Additional benefits of rest helps improve and increase concentration, ability to make sound decisions, and overall emotions and mood.

When you have worked all day, all you can think of is resting. To rest means to recover strength, or to refresh and start over. Work has a way of making you weary in well-being and testy when you have nothing left to give. Moments of rest are important because they capture the true essence of what life is about. We are required to recover strength, determined to discover new themes, and to reshape life's perspective toward our next great big adventure. Next time your mind, body, or soul is weary, take a rest and rejuvenate.

Back in 2014 my godmother blessed me with this good
advice, "Mr. Damon, when you work hard you always
want to remember:

- Take your lunch breaks, everyday!
- Set aside additional funds for retirement!
- Every 60 or 90 days take a 3-day weekend and try
  something *new.*"

Confession

Since that moment in 2014, I implemented her three tips and
have not looked back. I find time to take lunch at work even if
it is walking around the building once or twice or locking my
computer screen and sitting in silence! Moreover, I learned the
importance of a work-life balance. Real-life and work-life are
always a balancing act, and often times one wins more times
over the other. The idea of work-life balance means that we
must determine how to split our time and energy, all while being
functional and successful at both. In the last six or so years, I
incorporated the practice of work hard/play hard to understand
and balance work-life. 'Work hard' means to remain engaged long
enough to complete the essential functions of your job. 'Play hard'
intends to find the time and shift your energies toward something
that helps you regain strength.

For instance, I would spend ten or more hours working on a
grant application, but I would also find time to try a new chicken
recipe.

1. How do you define 'rest'?

2. When you rest, are you reducing noise? Spending time alone?

STEPHANIES OF THE WORLD

Stephanies of the world come in diverse fashions, yet, they are congruent in thought, action, and word. In other words, they are different people, but they all have the same thought and behavior patterns. Take for instance, the Stephanie at your previous job who always shared her relationship woes, financial mishaps, and would always complain about the boss and colleagues. You decided to leave that organization to later find another Stephanie in your new work setting. When people have this type of behavior, take it at face value, assess their reasoning, build your case, and store it for future use. The future use helps you determine how to work with and manage them going forward. Although there may be Stephanies of the world, just know you will grow stronger, wiser, and better.

Scenario

Stephanie is the co-worker that shares all of her personal life, i.e. she met her new boyfriend off a dating app, she pays $549 for her leased luxury vehicle, how her one friend keeps borrowing money from her, with you and those who are listening. You are trying to be a team player, so you listen and provide little to some feedback. Stephanie is upset with you because you are not reciprocating by spilling all of your personal information. Are you wrong? What do you do next?

SHADOW LEADERSHIP

You are always the person everyone comes to for help with a task or motivation because stress is mounting up and they have no one or nowhere else to turn to. You become more involved with their life, their decisions, and you spend less time with your own. In this instance, what do you do next? Stop sharing your help? Allow them to motivate themselves? This reminds me of the time during shift change when my former colleague would not only arrive late, they would spend nearly 15 to 20 minutes sharing their life situations and problems. I found myself offering unsolicited feedback, giving sound advice with next steps, and sharing with them more than what I bargained for. After several late arrivals, I decided to spend time and really address the behavior of arriving late to work, pouring out their emotions, and how it would leave me confused and bewildered. From that moment forward I felt freer from these unwelcomed distractions and our professional relationship grew and my colleague became stronger so they started their own business.

Scenario

Everyone goes to Helen for help. People know when you talk with Helen about your problem she will solve it for you. The issue is Helen would turn around and tell everyone else and your boss what she did for you. Is that wrong of her? What can you do differently next time before going to Helen?

STUCK WHERE THEY BELONG

Have you ever found yourself in a workplace or department where you felt you have outgrown the environment but are unsure about where to go next? But you stay! Do you remain there because you feel you have to? I was in a high paying job and knew the longer I stayed, the more miserable I would become; however, my goal was to keep working there to save money. Stuck where you belong is a mindset, an unmet reality. You were told because of your performance you were next in line for a promotion, yet it never surfaced. Maybe it happened two summers ago when you took on a few additional projects with the assumption you would get some credit during the presentation to later find out your teammate did the opposite. Being stuck is not a physical concept, rather, an intellectual one. People have a tough time identifying your triggers, so they create concepts they know will keep you producing good work.

Confession

Admittedly, to work at a place and know you are stuck for many reasons, such as age, race or gender, is hard. What makes being stuck most unrewarding is when you are told to keep up the great work, you have a bright future, but you know it is not at that job. The idea of being stuck in a job or place happened to me when I was a teenager. I worked for a place where people were given misleading information from management around products they were told to sell in order for the business to make a profit. Back then, I was naive and did not know what to do until my mother told me to "Do you and forget them." To me, it meant there was no need to compromise your integrity, quit the job, and let them hire someone else. Today, this same advice from my mother resonates with me just about every day. I have been in several stuck places, however, after spending time on the stair landing and listening to the hallway whispers, I later would make the sound decision and move on. Thanks Mom for this sound, tried and true advice!

JEFF AND PATS OF THE WORLD

Diversity and inclusion are important and necessary in the workplace today. Most organizations do not allow individuals to have space to be the best version of themselves because of unwritten rules and policies in the workplace. Diversity and inclusion are the fabrics needed to improve performance, morale, and individuality at work. Therefore, the workplace requires more people to see diversity in others and embrace it. Generally, the Jeff and Pats of the world see what potential looks like and encourage the unexpected, challenge the impossibilities, and guide the goals. Jeffs and Pats are the executive leaders that lead with a 'People First' mentality. They are not afraid to challenge the normal and find genuine ways to lead people in the right direction and ensure diversity is for all and no one is left out.

Diversity in the workplace is more than color, sex, and age; it involves education, experience, and the ability to empower others. Think about the boss whom you consider to be your best boss. What qualities does he or she possess that affords him or her the 'Best Boss' title? Was it the way they built you up? How did they see the world differently? Jeff and Pats of the world were the bridge leaders that helped spread diversity across the organizations they led. They went over and above to encourage diversity in thought, diversity in people, and diversity in changing the status quo. They spent a considerable amount of time understanding the difference people can make when you lead with diverse intentions.

Because of their diversity in leadership, I learned their ability to rally people together during uncertain times, embrace challenges, and use obstacles as lessons learned were some impressive qualities I recall and have implemented in my work as a leader. Either now or going forward, try not to allow people to refuse your diversity to dictate your divine destiny. You are equipped with the ability to see the world differently, so your perspective will encourage others to do the same thing. When you show up, others will too.

Confession

I learned the importance of building diverse teams and how integral doing so is for morale, performance, and my leadership. The Jeffs and Pats of the world allowed me to develop an appreciation for and understanding of the essentials of leading people with passion, integrity, diversity, and inclusion.

1.   How diverse is your department, team, or organization? How would you incorporate diversity in your workplace?

2.   Do you believe that diversity helps performance in the workplace? Why or why not?

3.   At present, who in your job would be considered the Jeff and Pats of the world? How do you know?

LEAD THE DANCE

There are times when you must take the initiative and lead the discussion, project, or new initiative. You have proven yourself that your leadership style helped rally everyone together and complete the task flawlessly. Jules, a colleague, is an up-and-coming emerging leader who seemingly leads people unknowingly. Her presence is electrifying. She commands the room when she enters. Others are always talking about how well she leads and manages her team and the projects she leads.

When you lead in those moments, you are dancing, just like Jules. Dancing is much like leadership; you are in action, and those around you can see. Your movements are met with the right decisions, your motives are motivating to others, and everything you seem to touch turns out better than before! You are in the groove. Your dance is electrifying! You are hyping others up! Overall, your leadership is creating a positive vibe that others recognize and want to join. Be willing to adjust your style and pace based on the employees, environment, and mission and understand that the song may change routinely.

Confession

You just joined Rosie's team as a middle manager. Right away, you learned the team's dynamics are really impressive; however, you noticed that one person does not agree with Jules' leadership style. They believe she is naive. She does not spend enough time managing certain projects. And, you learned that you were hired for the same position this staff member interviewed for. How would you lead this dance? What are your next steps?

PICKING UP HYMN BOOKS

A hymn book is a collection of songs composed and written by different people. The songs are more than words on paper. You find yourself humming the words in some of your most stressful moments. I remember as a teenager in the choir at church we learned how to hold the book properly, read the table of contents, find the song and pitch, and be prepared to sing when asked. This childhood memory created this everyday experience I find most useful when I am under the most stress at work.

A trusted advisor once offered great counsel and guidance when she told me to find my happy place when I am upset. Her happy place was swimming or painting pictures. Mine was choir rehearsal as a child (no, I cannot sing, let alone hold a note!). Whenever work stressors would pull me in multiple ways, I would remember Tuesday night choir rehearsal. The action of picking up the book was the strategy that helped me redefine my direction, consider how to move forward, be prepared with my decision, and move on!

Activity

In your workspace, consider what makes up your happy place and determine what it does for you. Be sure to share where you have seen this at play and how it equipped you to handle those stressful moments.

DOES YOUR BARK
MATCH YOUR BITE?

The adage 'a dog does not bark at parked cars' is vital for this everyday experience.' What does that mean to you? Most notably, dogs are not easily amused, nor do they get excited by parked cars. Parked cars are not the threat; the moving ones pose a danger. This everyday experience is engaged to educate us not to be easily consumed by the moving cars unless your bark matches your bite. Have you ever encountered someone that was all talk and no action? Did you have the boss that would talk more and work less? In those instances, what should we do? Keep silent? Share our discontent?

Confession

There was a time right after undergrad I started working for a boss that would bark orders, demand results, and rarely would put any thing to action. For example, instead of relaying information to the team, she would reprimand staff in front of everyone. This vexed me so much that one day I expressed my disdain and that changes needed to be made or I would have no other choice but to resign. To my dismay, nothing changed and I resigned two months later. In this confession, my bark matched my bite. I expressed how I felt and because there was no change I resigned. For many people to resign is not as easy as it was for me. If this were me today, I would rationalize their actions, understand where they are coming from, meet with the supervisor to discuss my concerns, and work toward an amicable agreement. Years later, I learned that when I would lead a team of people or a project I would ensure my bark (words) matched my bite (actions).

- From experience, what are some best ways to move from talk to action?

THE NURSE

In most cases, leaders in the workplace are like nurses in the hospital. Generally, a nurse is an individual that helps gather important health-related information before a doctor provides a diagnosis to help remedy the proposed health concern. In the workplace, a leader conducts a needs assessment, determines gaps in service delivery, creates viable options for improvement, and solicits feedback and updates throughout. Similarity, a nurse speaks on behalf of the patient by sharing symptoms, pain, or pressure so the doctor may understand the total picture. Much like this example, in the workplace, the leader is the nurse and helps paint the picture for those that require an added voice of reason on a project, when making a decision, and establishing your professional voice in meetings.

Next time when you encounter someone that cannot speak or think for themselves they would expect people like you and me to step in, step up, and speak on their behalf. Regardless of where you are and what you do, speak up, show up, and be the voice for someone else. Never allow someone to stifle your voice, rather, be the voice of reason and hope. Remember, someone is always counting on you. If not you, then who?

Scenario

Andrew is great at collecting and analyzing data. Because of this, Andrew's statements are always cut off or cut short by his immediate supervisor during every conference call. You can tell Andrew is getting defeated by the way he answers the questions when asked. You believe Andrew is being treated unfairly and you consider speaking with your boss about this situation. Because of your willingness to support his claims and your friendship with your boss, you decided to speak with her. During the discussion you sense that your boss does not agree with your comments and disagrees with you. What should you do next?

CURVE BALLS

In our workspace, we are often thrown several curve balls at any given moment. Just like in baseball, your opponent attempts to throw curve balls to keep you from hitting the ball and a homerun. Same with life, it expects us to take each ball, place it in its proper place, and move on. Don't you wish managing and removing curve balls were that easy? On the contrary, work and life's curve balls come in many shapes, sizes, situations, spaces, and seasons. We must manage those curve balls as they are thrown.

Moving up the due date for a project or rewriting the grant application that was mistakenly deleted and not saved are examples of curve balls in the workplace. These curveballs may be tragedies or trials that later turn into our testimonies. Tragedies are those moments that tend to knock us off our game, yet we pull ourselves together and do what we can with what little strength we have left in us. Trials are moments in time where your endurance is tried while others are looking on to see what you decide to do next. Always remember that winners win! Losses are lessons waiting on us to learn from. At work, in our home, or on the sports team we are always being thrown curve balls to knock us off the right path.

Regardless of the curve ball, be sure you understand what was expected, let it go, and move on. Curve balls are supposed to confuse, blindside, or mature you. When you understand what was meant to happen, you will learn the lesson and let it go. Letting something go does not mean you forget. You are not bitter about the situation, you are better. That is why you need to move on. Moving on means you are going forward with the hope of not returning.

WITH CHALLENGE COMES PAIN

I really enjoy hearing stories about how my parents grew up. Although their stories are more personal than professional, I can still take away nuggets of wisdom. In an earlier experience I shared my mother told me years ago to 'Do me and forget them.' This stemmed from her growing up in a predominately non-diverse neighborhood. She learned rather quickly, in order to be different and be who she was, she could not allow others' ideas and behaviors to affect her. Along the same lines, my father grew up without his father because he died when he was a teenager. He always told me to do things in life to make him proud. In each of their challenges, I learned that their pain allowed them to grow up and mature sooner than they needed to. These two moments with my parents allowed me to understand that with challenges comes pain in the workplace and I must use it to grow my thinking and my voice. In order to be an effective leader and a voice for change, I must be the resilient, transformative, and thoughtful person to lead with integrity, character, and make my parents proud.

Challenges give you the clarity that you need to stop, look, and learn. You stop to analyze the situation. You look for alternative solutions. And, you learn what will work and how it will be presented. Challenges allow the pain to help us endure those 'what ifs' in life and offers us that uncomfortable feeling that makes us want to move and be different. Next time pain comes, be sure to be the victor over it and not victim; just like my mother and father. Instead of walling in those uncomfortable feelings, stop what you are doing, look for another way to handle it, and learn from the experience.

When you use the stop, look, and listen tip you will always come out the victor.

With this image, how would you describe this to a colleague? What work project would you use to drive home your point?

CHINA SCALE
EXPERIENCE

In June 2016 I was offered a teaching and supervising role in
Beijing, China. When I arrived, I was not prepared to handle the
many obstacles thrown at me. What sticks out most was my first
interaction on the Beijing subway. I was so nervous because the
signs were written in Mandarin. I did not have the interpreter
there to help me, and it was my first day on the job. I froze! I
cried! And then, I learned rather quickly that being timid in
unknown places will not get me far. I noticed that traffic moves
faster when I am standing still. I realized moving to another
country that my barriers did not leave, they multiplied. Because
of my China scale experience, I pondered on what I learned from
that subway obstacle and how it would later help me in certain
workplace situations. These underlined experiences help me now
when making on the spot decisions and the effects they may have
on others on my team.

Although experiences like this do not happen often, there are
instances in your life that you may use as an experience for
learning.

There are times in our professional life where widespread negative
or emotional behaviors require immediate change of direction,
space, or company. Political upheaval, an aggressive colleague, the

'we have always done it this way' mindset, or workplace bullying are those professional concerns that require immediate changes, would you agree? Too often we allow nouns (persons, places, things) to take control or live rent free in our minds and hope for a different outcome. When you are confronted with a similar experience as stated above, consider the following:

- understand the behavior
- come up with two possible solutions
- act with caution but with immediacy
- and never turn back

JODYS ON THE JOB

When you first arrive on the job you are looking for people to connect with to ease your workplace jitters. You instantly connect with Jody. She appears friendly, helpful, and willing to share work politics and advises whom to watch out for and what not to do. Over time, you use what the Jodys offer to help you navigate negative people and poor behaviors. However, the Jodys realize that you are learning much too quickly in her estimation. They notice you do not need them as much, so they stop sharing everything with you.

This experience happened to me while I was in China. The language and cultural barriers were not the only challenges I had; it was also navigating some of my colleagues. Once I learned the "players" at work, I no longer needed to rely on their information. Instead, I used my knowledge to maneuver through the workplace. I found that this strategy bothered some of my colleagues and instead of bringing their concerns to my attention, they gossiped about it with one another.

The most feasible way, at the time, was to speak with them about the concerns and part ways from the organization, instead of working towards a solution. Had I known the 'Head-on Collision' everyday experience, I would have used my night vision to under stand their perspective. Hindsight has taught me that I could have applied the Head-on Collision experience by using my night vision to understand and appreciate their perspective.

1. How do you overcome or manage a Jody on the job?

2. In your current or previous workplace, what did you do to overcome Jodys on the job?

WALKING WELL

You are always positive, uplifting, and encouraging to yourself and those around you. To walk well means to be fit to respond to answers with ease and care. To walk well means you are prepared to be okay with the answer and know how to move forward. When you walk well your decorum is seen and noticed by others, in essence, they see you always striving to do the right thing at all times. Next time, be the well-walker.

Confession

Wyatt is wise beyond his years. He is 28 years old and recently graduated with his Master's in Business Administration. He is always dressed to impress. He arrives to work on time and leaves when it is time to go. Wyatt works well with others and tries to see all perspectives before sharing his feedback. Because of his personality traits and workplace performance, Wyatt was promoted to team lead on the job. If we had more Wyatt's at work, would morale increase? Would the team meet performance goals and objectives?

THE SIGNAL

We often see signs of distress, discomfort, or distractions way before they become a mountain. The reason we choose not to trust our instinct and make change is because we focus on the signals and not the sign. The signals are often displayed when you make careless mistakes such as not finishing a project and leaving it for someone else or taking on more than you need to. The signal is the blinking light that says "caution, stand back." The sign is the large, red octagon saying "stop" or "do not enter." Signals may appear in an "aha!" moment with a colleague, when difficult tasks become much easier or reading one of the everyday experiences. When given a signal, attempt to trust what it is tailored to teach you, make connections with it, and determine how best to develop skills and traits to manage it or ways to break it and overcome it. I can recall a time where I noticed the signs of a direct report could not complete the essential functions of his job. Instead of getting frustrated (red) and emotional over his poor performance, I met with him to understand what areas he is struggling in that prohibits him from completing his everyday tasks (yellow). Once we learned his signs, we were able to improve his signal and with time he not only mastered his everyday tasks, he would later grow into a new role (green).

Which color represents your current state at work? How are you managing these matters?

COLOR	SIGNAL	EVERYDAY EXPERIENCE TO CONSIDER
RED	Easily angered, often frustrated, quick tempered, or emotional	Moments of Rest
YELLOW	Tough to finish small projects, requiring more time to finish normal tasks	China Scale Experience
GREEN	Upbeat, encouraging, projects finishing timely	Walking Well

• Draw your version of a traffic signal and write the words joy, peace, and patience inside each shape that represents a signal.

• Next, jot down whether you agree joy, peace, and patience are essentially equal in order to balance work and life.

• After that, create a 15-second video and explain this everyday experience and your illustration with someone.

ABOUT THE AUTHOR

Dr. Gary Damon Jr., a native of Buffalo, New York, and current president of Pressure Point Consulting, LLC, a leading boutique consulting firm that offers workforce training, grant development, and emerging leader and executive coaching. Dr. Damon worked in diverse sectors across the world in leadership roles in the last decade. He has lived in Philadelphia, Pennsylvania, Beijing, China, and currently resides in Memphis, Tennessee. Dr. Damon works to build positive, long-lasting relationships with people he may encounter. With his quick wit, boisterous attitude, and upfront motivation, he encourages everyone to be better than the day before. He uses his motto "I seek to leave things better than before" in just about anything he does. Dr. Damon is a jet-setter and has traveled across the world but is grounded locally and enjoys local eateries and coffee shops.

"Everyday Experiences" is a very clever "how to" book to have employees and managers reflect on their work to improve self and team performance. Gary, I really like your everyday metaphors of the stair landing, closet, etc. All will be easily relatable to your audience.

-Dr. Tim Hartigan, Owner, TJH5Consulting